TEST YOUR BRIDGE TECHNIQUE

ENTRY
MANAGEMENT

D0743531

David Bird
Tim Bourke

MASTER POINT PRESS • TORONTO

Master Point Press
331 Douglas Ave.
Toronto, Ontario, Canada
M5M 1H2
(416) 781-0351
Website: http://www.masterpointpress.com
Email: info@masterpointpress.com

Library and Archives Canada Cataloguing in Publication

Bird, David, 1946-
       Entry management / David Bird & Tim Bourke.

(Test your bridge technique)
ISBN 1-894154-75-4

       1. Contract bridge. I. Bourke, Tim I. Title. III. Series: Bird, David, 1946- . Test your bridge technique.

GV1282.435.B57 2004   795.41'53   C2004-904597-0

Editor   Ray Lee
Cover and interior design   Olena S. Sullivan/New Mediatrix
Interior format and copy editing   Luise Lee

Printed in Canada by Webcom Ltd.

1 2 3 4 5 6 7   09 08 07 06 05 04

INTRODUCTION

This book is designed to accompany *Entry Management*, Book #1 in the *Bridge Technique series*. It will give you the opportunity to practice playing in contracts where special attention has to be paid to the entry situation.

Before the problems section starts we have included a brief review of some of the techniques required to create extra entries. These may suffice for solving some of the early problems in the book. Later on, more advanced techniques will be required. Don't worry if you fail to spot the winning line of play when you first attempt a problem. The necessary technique will be clearly explained in the solution that follows.

Whether you find the problems in this book a gentle jog or a hard slog, we are sure you will enjoy the journey. Next time you face such situations at the table you will be much more likely to spot the solution.

HOW TO MANAGE YOUR ENTRIES

Entry management ensures that you are in the right hand at the right time and is an important part of planning the play of a hand. It may involve special techniques within a single suit — to create extra entries or to avoid blockages that would kill a necessary entry.

One such technique is needed on this deal:

```
              ♠ 9 4 3
              ♡ A J 9 3
              ◇ J 10 9
              ♣ 6 5 2
♠ 6 2                        ♠ K 8 7 5
♡ 10 8 6 5       N          ♡ 2
◇ 7 4 2       W     E       ◇ 8 6 5 3
♣ 10 9 8 4       S          ♣ A J 7 3
              ♠ A Q J 10
              ♡ K Q 7 4
              ◇ A K Q
              ♣ K Q
```

You arrive in 6♡ and West leads the ♣10 to his partner's ace. Back comes a club and you win in your hand. The next move is obvious. Yes, you stop to make a plan! To avoid losing a spade trick, you will need to find East with the ♠K. That's not the end of the story, though. If East holds four or more spades, you will need three entries to dummy so that you can take three spade finesses.

After winning the second round of clubs, you should draw one round of trumps with the king. When you lead the ♡Q at Trick 4, West follows suit. It is then safe to overtake with dummy's ♡A. By overtaking the queen with the ace, you promote the value of dummy's jack and nine of hearts. In fact you promote them into the second and third entries that you need to the dummy.

East shows out on the second round of trumps but this causes no problem. You finesse the ♠Q and justice is done (your opponents may not agree) when the finesse wins. You return to dummy by taking a marked finesse of the ♡9 and repeat the spade finesse. Finally you cross to dummy's ♡J and finesse yet again in spades. East did indeed hold ♠K-x-x-x, so your elegant maneuver in the trump suit proved to be necessary.

Sometimes entry management is just a fancy name for making plays in the right order. When you need to set up a side suit in dummy, it may be necessary to use the entries that dummy's trump holding provides.

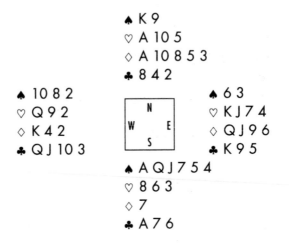

```
              ♠ K 9
              ♡ A 10 5
              ◇ A 10 8 5 3
              ♣ 8 4 2
♠ 10 8 2                        ♠ 6 3
♡ Q 9 2          N             ♡ K J 7 4
◇ K 4 2      W       E         ◇ Q J 9 6
♣ Q J 10 3       S             ♣ K 9 5
              ♠ A Q J 7 5 4
              ♡ 8 6 3
              ◇ 7
              ♣ A 7 6
```

West leads the ♣Q against your contract of 4♠. (3NT would have been more sensible, yes, but you like a challenge.) You win with the ♣A and see that you have two heart losers and two club losers staring you in the face. How should you play the contract?

The only chance to dispose of a loser is to establish dummy's diamond suit. Since you will have to take three diamond ruffs and then return to dummy to enjoy the long card, you will need four entries to the dummy. The red aces will give you two entries. The other two entries will have to come from the trump suit and this will mean taking an 'unnecessary finesse'.

After winning the club lead, you cross to the ◇A and ruff a diamond. You then, very casually, play a spade to the nine. Yes — the finesse wins! A second diamond ruff is followed by a trump to the king and a third diamond ruff with a high trump. Now all that remains is to draw West's last trump and to cross to the ♡A. You can then discard one of your losers on the established card in diamonds. If West had made an inspired opening lead in one of the majors, this would have killed the contract.

Sometimes the only entry management that is needed is to win the opening lead in the right hand. An inexperienced player might go wrong on this deal:

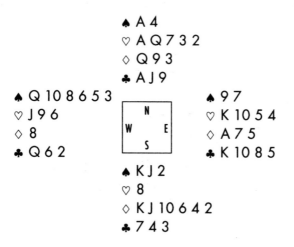

```
                    ♠ A 4
                    ♡ A Q 7 3 2
                    ◇ Q 9 3
                    ♣ A J 9
♠ Q 10 8 6 5 3                      ♠ 9 7
♡ J 9 6              N              ♡ K 10 5 4
◇ 8            W          E         ◇ A 7 5
♣ Q 6 2             S               ♣ K 10 8 5
                    ♠ K J 2
                    ♡ 8
                    ◇ K J 10 6 4 2
                    ♣ 7 4 3
```

West leads the ♠6 against 3NT. You win in your hand with the ♠J and pause to make a plan. Do you? It's too late! When you play on the diamond suit East will hold up his ace until the third round. With no entry to the South hand you will score only two diamond tricks. There will be no way to recover.

The right time to make a plan is *before* your first play from dummy. Here you have four top cards outside the diamond suit. By adding five diamond winners to this total, you will make the game easily. To guarantee an entry to the established diamond winners, you should win the opening lead with dummy's ♠A. It will then make no difference if East holds up the diamond ace for two rounds. When you regain the lead, you will be able to cross to the South hand with the ♠K.

Let's look next at some plays that aim to avoid a blockage in a suit. Would you have seen the danger on the next deal?

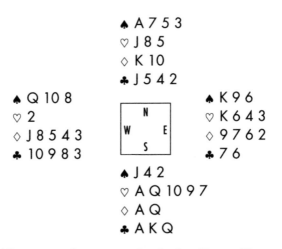

Overbidding somewhat, you arrive in 6♡. How will you play this contract when West leads the ♣10?

You have two potential losers in spades and one in the trump suit. You must aim to throw one spade loser on dummy's fourth club and to pick up the trump suit without loss by finessing against East's king. (You hope it will be East's king, anyway.)

You win the club lead in your hand and cross to dummy by overtaking the ♢Q with the ♢K. Suppose your next move is to lead the ♡J, playing the ♡7 from your hand when East does not cover. You will go down. The finesse will win but when you repeat the finesse you will have to win in the South hand. There is only one entry to the dummy left (the ♠A) and you cannot afford to use that for a third trump finesse. That's because the final entry will be needed to score the ♣J after that suit has been unblocked.

So, when you lead the ♡J at Trick 3 you should follow with the ♡10 or ♡9 from your hand. You can then lead the ♡8, playing the ♡7 from your hand. *The lead will still be in dummy.* You take a third finesse in hearts and draw East's last trump. It will then be a simple matter to cash the remaining two club winners in your hand and to enter dummy with the ♠A to cash the ♣J. Away will go one of your spade losers and the slam is yours.

As a final example of managing your entries carefully we will look at the common technique of winning a trick with a higher card than is necessary. Your aim is to promote a lesser card in the dummy into an entry.

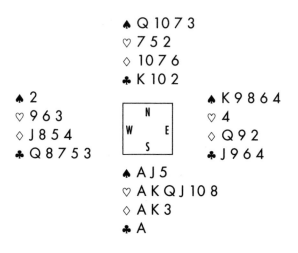

West leads the ♠2 against your small slam in hearts. Perhaps you think that no harm can be done by playing the ♠10 from dummy. Do that and you will go down! East knows that the opening lead is either a singleton or (less likely) from ♠J-5-2. In neither case can there be any benefit in playing his king. He will play low and — twist and turn as you may — you will then go down, losing one spade and one diamond (or a ruff and a diamond if you attempt a spade finesse at Trick 2).

To make the slam you must not only play low from dummy on the first trick, you must also win the ace. No further magic is required. You will draw trumps, play the ♣A and lead the ♠5 to dummy's ♠10. Whether or not East takes his ♠K on this round, you will gain access to the dummy and take a diamond discard on the ♣K.

Exactly the same play is required, of course, if West has led a spade from K-x-x-x. Unless you win the first trick with the ace, West can prevent you from gaining access to the dummy.

In this introductory chapter we have looked at a few basic ideas involving entry management. In the thirty-six problems that follow you will be able to test your own ability, to see whether you are adept at handling entries. Don't worry if you find some of the problems a bit tricky. After reading the answer, and our explanation of the winning play, such deals will become very much easier in the future. Good luck!

Problem 1

　　　　　　　　♠ K Q J 10 4
　　　　　　　　♡ 7 2
　　　　　　　　◇ A K 5
　　　　　　　　♣ 10 9 6

◇J led

　　　　　　　　♠ A 5 2
　　　　　　　　♡ K 5
　　　　　　　　◇ 7 6 2
　　　　　　　　♣ A K Q 8 4

WEST	NORTH	EAST	SOUTH
			1NT
pass	2♡*	pass	2♠
pass	3NT	pass	4♣
pass	4◇	pass	4♡
pass	6♠	all pass	

How will you play the spade slam when West leads the ◇J?

Problem 2

　　　　　　　　♠ 4 2
　　　　　　　　♡ A 5 3 2
　　　　　　　　◇ A 8 6 5
　　　　　　　　♣ Q J 5

♡10 led

　　　　　　　　♠ A Q J 7
　　　　　　　　♡ K Q J 7 6
　　　　　　　　◇ Q 2
　　　　　　　　♣ A 4

WEST	NORTH	EAST	SOUTH
			1♡
pass	3♡	pass	3♠
pass	4◇	pass	4NT
pass	5♡*	pass	6♡
all pass			

West leads the ♡10 against 6♡. How will you play the contract?

Problem 3 ●●●

♠ J 10 3 2
♡ 8 7 4 3
◇ 10 7 5 3
♣ 6

◇ 2 led

♠ A Q
♡ A K Q 10 9
◇ A K 6 4
♣ A K

WEST	NORTH	EAST	SOUTH
			2♣
pass	2◇	pass	2♡
pass	4♡	pass	6♡
all pass			

West leads the ◇2 against your heart slam. How will you play?

Problem 4 ●●

♠ 9 7 5 4
♡ 10 8 3
◇ 4 3
♣ Q J 10 3

◇ 6 led

♠ A K 6 3
♡ A K Q J 9 7 2
◇ A K
♣ —

WEST	NORTH	EAST	SOUTH
			2♣
pass	2◇	pass	2♡
pass	2NT	pass	3♠
pass	4♡	pass	6♡
all pass			

West leads the ◇6 against 6♡. How will you plan the play?

```
                    ♠ K Q J 10 4
                    ♡ 7 2
                    ♢ A K 5
                    ♣ 10 9 6
    ♠ 9 8 7 3                          ♠ 6
    ♡ A 10 4 3          N              ♡ Q J 9 8 6
    ♢ J 10 9 3      W       E          ♢ Q 8 4
    ♣ 5                 S              ♣ J 7 3 2
                    ♠ A 5 2
                    ♡ K 5
                    ♢ 7 6 2
                    ♣ A K Q 8 4
```

WEST	NORTH	EAST	SOUTH
			1NT
pass	2♡*	pass	2♠
pass	3NT	pass	4♣
pass	4♢	pass	4♡
pass	6♠	all pass	

Your 4♣ cuebid agrees spades as trumps and shows a hand that is suitable for slam play. How will you play 6♠ when West leads the ♢J?

If you can score a full five club tricks, this will bring the total to twelve. There will be no problem if clubs break 3-2. You will have to avoid a blockage, though, if East started with ♣J-x-x-x. Win the diamond lead and draw trumps in four rounds. Now lead the ♣10 to your ♣A. By removing the ♣10 from the scene, you are part-way towards preparing for a finesse of your ♣8. Next you cash the ♣K, following with the ♣9 from dummy. West does indeed show out on this trick. You return to dummy with a diamond and lead the ♣6 to your ♣8. Five club tricks, and the slam, are yours.

If you had not retained your ♣6 to lead on the third round, dummy's ♣10 or ♣9 would have won that trick. With no certain entry to the remaining club winners, you would have had to risk everything on a lead towards the ♡K.

(If West started with ♣J-x-x-x, you will establish the clubs with a ruff and later lead towards the ♡K, hoping for the best.)

```
                      ♠ 4 2
                      ♡ A 5 3 2
                      ◇ A 8 6 5
                      ♣ Q J 5
     ♠ 10 8 5                          ♠ K 9 6 3
     ♡ 10 9 8          ┌─────────┐     ♡ 4
     ◇ K 9 7           │    N    │     ◇ J 10 4 3
     ♣ K 10 9 6        │ W     E │     ♣ 8 7 3 2
                       │    S    │
                       └─────────┘
                      ♠ A Q J 7
                      ♡ K Q J 7 6
                      ◇ Q 2
                      ♣ A 4
```

WEST	NORTH	EAST	SOUTH
			1♡
pass	3♡	pass	3♠
pass	4◇	pass	4NT
pass	5♡*	pass	6♡
all pass			

West leads the ♡10 against your small slam in hearts. It is almost certain that you will need the ♠K to be onside. How should you plan the play? In particular, how should you manage your entries to dummy, which are not plentiful?

Win the trump lead with the king and cross to the ace of trumps. You finesse the ♠Q, pleased to see the finesse win, and draw the last trump with the queen. What next? If you cross to the ◇A to repeat the spade finesse, you will go down. With a diamond loser exposed, you would have to take a successful club finesse to make the slam. Instead you should play ace and another club, setting up a second club trick for a diamond discard. You are then safe on any return. If West returns a club, for example, you will win and discard your diamond loser. You can then repeat the spade finesse and ruff your last spade in dummy.

```
            ♠ J 10 3 2
            ♡ 8 7 4 3
            ◇ 10 7 5 3
            ♣ 6
♠ K 9 7 5                    ♠ 8 6 4
♡ J 6 5          N           ♡ 2
◇ 2          W     E         ◇ Q J 9 8
♣ J 9 8 7 2      S           ♣ Q 10 5 4 3
            ♠ A Q
            ♡ A K Q 10 9
            ◇ A K 6 4
            ♣ A K
```

WEST	NORTH	EAST	SOUTH
			2♣
pass	2◇	pass	2♡
pass	4♡	pass	6♡
all pass			

West leads the ◇2 against your small slam in hearts and you win East's ◇8 with the ace. You then draw trumps in three rounds. What next?

It's not a difficult hand, once you see the answer. You must play the ace and queen of spades, setting up two spade winners in the dummy. You can then reach dummy by ruffing the second round of clubs, allowing you to discard the two diamond losers on the jack and ten of spades.

What if West attempts to thwart this plan by holding up the ♠K? Nice defensive effort, but it does not work on the present deal. Spared a loser in the spade suit, you can discard one of dummy's diamonds on the second round of clubs. Then, after king and another diamond, you will be able to ruff your last diamond in the dummy.

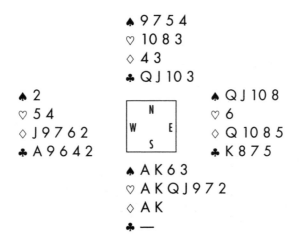

```
              ♠ 9 7 5 4
              ♡ 10 8 3
              ◊ 4 3
              ♣ Q J 10 3
  ♠ 2                              ♠ Q J 10 8
  ♡ 5 4           N               ♡ 6
  ◊ J 9 7 6 2   W   E             ◊ Q 10 8 5
  ♣ A 9 6 4 2     S               ♣ K 8 7 5
              ♠ A K 6 3
              ♡ A K Q J 9 7 2
              ◊ A K
              ♣ —
```

WEST	NORTH	EAST	SOUTH
			2♣
pass	2◊	pass	2♡
pass	2NT	pass	3♠
pass	4♡	pass	6♡
all pass			

West leads the ◊6 against 6♡. How will you plan the play?

One possibility is to win, draw trumps and hope that the spades break 3-2, but this is only a 68% chance. A better line is to take two ruffing finesses in clubs. Whenever East holds at least one of the top club honors, you can set up a club for your twelfth trick. Initially the chance that East holds at least one club honor is 74%. Since West would surely have led a club from the ♣A-K, the prospects soar to nearly 100%.

You will need three entries to the dummy — two to lead a club honor and one more to cash the club trick that you establish. Win the diamond lead and overtake your ♡9 with dummy's ♡10. When both defenders follow to the first heart, you know that you will have three entries to dummy. You lead the ♣Q and discard a spade from your hand. West wins with the ♣A and returns another diamond. You win in the South hand and lead the ♡7 to dummy's ♡8. When you lead the ♣J, East covers with the ♣K (if he chose not to, you would throw your last spade loser). You ruff high in the South hand and lead the ♡2 to dummy's ♡3. You throw the remaining spade loser on dummy's ♣10 and claim the contract.

Problem 5

```
                    ♠ A Q J 6
                    ♡ A Q J 8
                    ◇ 8 7
                    ♣ A K Q
  ◇ Q led
                    ♠ 10 9 5 4
                    ♡ K 5 4 2
                    ◇ A 5
                    ♣ J 8 5
```

WEST	NORTH	EAST	SOUTH
	2♣	pass	2NT
pass	3♣*	pass	3♡
pass	6♡	all pass	

West leads the ◇Q against your borderline slam in hearts. How will you give yourself the best chance?

Problem 6

```
                    ♠ A 7
                    ♡ A 7 2
                    ◇ K Q 9 7 6
                    ♣ A 10 6
  ♣ K led
                    ♠ K Q 8 4 3 2
                    ♡ K 3
                    ◇ A
                    ♣ 9 5 4 2
```

WEST	NORTH	EAST	SOUTH
			1♠
pass	2◇	pass	2♠
pass	3♣	pass	3♠
pass	6♠	all pass	

What is your plan for the spade slam when West leads the ♣K?

Problem 7

```
            ♠ J 7
            ♡ 9 2
            ◇ A K 3
            ♣ A 9 8 5 4 3
♣K led
            ♠ A 2
            ♡ A K Q J 7 5 3
            ◇ 7 5 2
            ♣ 7
```

WEST	NORTH	EAST	SOUTH
	1♣	pass	2♡
pass	3♣	pass	3♡
pass	4◇	pass	6♡
all pass			

West leads the ♣K against your heart slam. How will you play?

Problem 8

```
            ♠ A 6 3 2
            ♡ 7 4 2
            ◇ 5 2
            ♣ J 9 6 3
◇J led
            ♠ K Q J 9 7
            ♡ A Q 5
            ◇ A K
            ♣ Q 10 5
```

WEST	NORTH	EAST	SOUTH
			2NT
pass	3♣	pass	3♠
pass	4♠	all pass	

West leads the ◇J against your spade game. How will you play the contract?

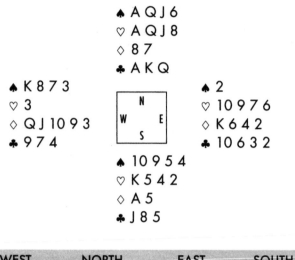

```
              ♠ A Q J 6
              ♡ A Q J 8
              ◇ 8 7
              ♣ A K Q
  ♠ K 8 7 3                    ♠ 2
  ♡ 3              N           ♡ 10 9 7 6
  ◇ Q J 10 9 3   W   E        ◇ K 6 4 2
  ♣ 9 7 4          S           ♣ 10 6 3 2
              ♠ 10 9 5 4
              ♡ K 5 4 2
              ◇ A 5
              ♣ J 8 5
```

WEST	NORTH	EAST	SOUTH
	2♣	pass	2NT
pass	3♣*	pass	3♡
pass	6♡	all pass	

West leads the ◇Q against your small slam in hearts. You and your partner are both minimum for your actions and you see straight away that you will need the ♠K to be onside. Is it time to move on to the next problem? Not quite! If West holds four spades including the king you will need to take three finesses in the suit. How will you manage the entries to the South hand?

Suppose you win the diamond lead and draw two rounds of trumps with the ace and queen, West showing out on the second round. You draw the remaining trumps with the jack and king and then lead the ♠10. West will not cover and your ten will win. When you repeat the finesse, you will have to win the trick in dummy. East will show out and there will be no way to repeat the spade finesse. Down one!

Once you foresee this problem it is not difficult to spot the solution. At Trick 2 you must take full advantage of being in the South hand. You must lead one of your low spades to dummy's queen. You then draw trumps in four rounds, ending in your hand. You can now lead the ♠10 on the second round of the suit. You run the card and East shows out. No matter. You are in the right hand to take a third spade finesse and you make the slam.

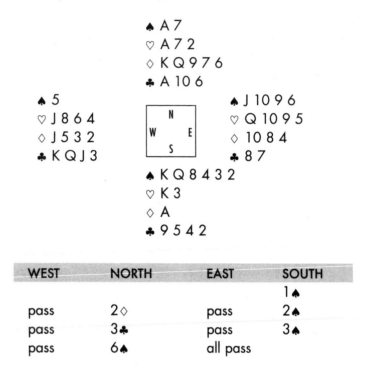

| A 7
| ♡ A 7 2
| ◊ K Q 9 7 6
| ♣ A 10 6

WEST	NORTH	EAST	SOUTH
			1♠
pass	2◊	pass	2♠
pass	3♣	pass	3♠
pass	6♠	all pass	

The bidding looks a bit questionable but there is nothing wrong with the final contract. How would you tackle the play when West leads the ♣K?

Since twelve tricks will be straightforward if trumps are 3-2, you should direct your energies towards some plan to overcome a 4-1 trump break. In that case you will need to discard all three of your club losers. Dummy's ◊ K-Q will provide two discards and you will have to set up a long diamond to provide the extra discard that you need.

To avoid entry problems, you must start on the rescue plan before you actually know that trumps are 4-1. Win the club lead and play a diamond to the ace. Then test the trump suit by playing the king and ace. If trumps break 3-2, return to the ♡K and simply draw the last trump.

When West shows out on the second trump, play the king and queen of diamonds, discarding two clubs. You then lead a fourth round of diamonds. It would do East no good to ruff from his natural trump trick as you would simply discard your last club. East discards, therefore, and you ruff in your hand. Now you return to dummy with the ♡A and lead the thirteenth diamond. Whether or not East chooses to ruff, you will discard your last club. Every entry to dummy was precious, as you see. If you had wasted the ♠A as an entry you would have gone down.

```
                    ♠ J 7
                    ♡ 9 2
                    ◇ A K 3
                    ♣ A 9 8 5 4 3
   ♠ K 9 5                        ♠ Q 10 8 6 4 3
   ♡ 10 6          N              ♡ 8 4
   ◇ Q 9 8 4    W     E           ◇ J 10 6
   ♣ K Q J 6       S              ♣ 10 2
                    ♠ A 2
                    ♡ A K Q J 7 5 3
                    ◇ 7 5 2
                    ♣ 7
```

WEST	NORTH	EAST	SOUTH
	1♣	pass	2♡
pass	3♣	pass	3♡
pass	4◇	pass	6♡
all pass			

The slam is a poor one, it's true, but if you can make twelve tricks there will be no need for a post-mortem on the bidding. West leads the ♣K. How will you tackle the play?

You have one loser in spades and another in diamonds and the only line that offers any real hope is to set up dummy's clubs. You win the opening lead with dummy's ace of clubs and ruff a club immediately, both defenders following. You then cross to the ◇A and ruff another club. If clubs had broken 3-3, you would have drawn trumps and re-entered dummy with a diamond. As it is, East shows out and you ruff with a high trump, preserving your ♡7-5.

Your only remaining chance is to find that trumps are 2-2 and West holds the ♡10. With this hope in mind, you lead a low trump towards dummy's ♡9. The defenders cannot defeat the contract now. Let's suppose that West rises with the ♡10 and returns a diamond. You win with dummy's ◊K and ruff another club to set up the suit. You return to dummy with the ♡9, drawing the defenders' trumps at the same time. You can then throw your spade and diamond losers on the two established clubs in dummy. (Just as well West didn't lead a spade, a diamond or the ♡6!)

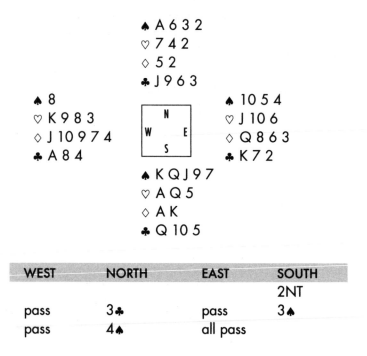

A 6 3 2
♡ 7 4 2
◊ 5 2
♣ J 9 6 3

♠ 8
♡ K 9 8 3
◊ J 10 9 7 4
♣ A 8 4

♠ 10 5 4
♡ J 10 6
◊ Q 8 6 3
♣ K 7 2

♠ K Q J 9 7
♡ A Q 5
◊ A K
♣ Q 10 5

WEST	NORTH	EAST	SOUTH
			2NT
pass	3♣	pass	3♠
pass	4♠	all pass	

West leads the ◊J against your spade game and you win in the South hand. You have two potential losers in hearts and two certain losers in clubs. How can you reduce the total of four losers to three? One possibility is to take a heart finesse. This relies on luck and you would much rather discard a heart loser on dummy's long card in the club suit.

Suppose you draw trumps with the ace, king and queen. Against accurate defense you will now go down. When you lead the ♣Q, the defenders will allow this to win. You cash the other top diamond and play another club, but the defenders now take the ace and king, allowing East to exit with the ♡J. Since the ♠A has not been preserved as an entry to dummy, there will be no way to reach the established club there.

Instead you should draw trumps with the king, queen and jack. You cash the other high diamond and lead the ♣Q. If East wins the first or second round of clubs with the king and switches to the ♡J, you rise with the ♡A. When West wins with the ♣A he will not be able to continue hearts profitably and the game is yours.

Suppose instead that West wins the first club and exists safely in clubs. When East wins the third round of clubs and switches to the ♡J, you can seek an overtrick by finessing the ♡Q. Ten tricks are assured because the ♠A will be an entry to the established winner in clubs. You can therefore discard your remaining heart loser.

Problem 9 ···

             ♠ 8 7 3 2
             ♡ Q 7 4 2
             ◇ A 7
             ♣ 8 5 4

♡K led

             ♠ K Q J 10 9 4
             ♡ 6
             ◇ K 8 3
             ♣ A Q 2

WEST	NORTH	EAST	SOUTH
			1♠
2♡	2♠	pass	4♠
all pass			

West leads the ♡K against your spade game. He then switches to ace and another trump. How will you play your contract?

Problem 10 ···

             ♠ Q 8 5
             ♡ J 5
             ◇ 10 4
             ♣ K Q J 5 3 2

♠4 led

             ♠ K 10 6
             ♡ A K 6 2
             ◇ A K 8
             ♣ 10 9 4

WEST	NORTH	EAST	SOUTH
			1NT
pass	3NT	all pass	

West leads the ♠4 against 3NT, East playing the ♠9. How will you play?

Problem 11

```
                    ♠ 7 5 4
                    ♡ 4 3
                    ◇ Q 8 6 5
                    ♣ A K 6 5
    ◇9 led
                    ♠ A K Q J 10
                    ♡ K 8
                    ◇ A K 7 4
                    ♣ 10 4
```

WEST	NORTH	EAST	SOUTH
		2♡*	dbl
pass	3♣*	pass	3♠
pass	4♠	pass	4NT
pass	5◇*	pass	6♠
all pass			

West leads the ◇9 against your spade slam. How will you play the contract?

Problem 12

```
                    ♠ J 9 7
                    ♡ 8 5 2
                    ◇ K 7 2
                    ♣ 10 6 4 2
    ♠4 led
                    ♠ K 6 5
                    ♡ A Q 3
                    ◇ A 6 5
                    ♣ A Q J 5
```

WEST	NORTH	EAST	SOUTH
			2NT
pass	3NT	all pass	

West leads the ♠4 against 3NT, East winning with the ace. What is your plan for the contract?

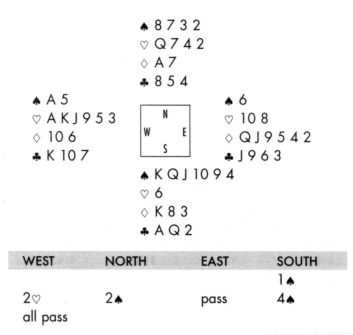

WEST	NORTH	EAST	SOUTH
			1♠
2♡	2♠	pass	4♠
all pass			

West leads the ♡K against your spade game. He then switches to ace and another trump. How will you play your contract?

The general line of play should be to eliminate diamonds and to throw in West with the fourth round of hearts, discarding the ♣2 from your hand. West will then have to lead a club into the A-Q tenace or give you a ruff-and-sluff.

Since you need to ruff two hearts in your hand you must be careful with your entries to the dummy. At Trick 2, when West cashes the ace of trumps, you must drop the ♠9 from your hand. You can then win the trump continuation with dummy's ♠8 and ruff a heart. Returning to dummy with the ♢A, you ruff another heart. You then reach dummy for the third time by cashing the ♢K and ruffing a diamond.

Finally, you lead the ♡Q and discard the ♣2 from your hand. You have only black cards left in both your hand and the dummy. The great moment has arrived and you survey this end position:

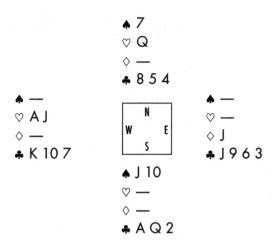

You lead the ♡Q from dummy and discard the ♣2 from your hand. West wins with the ♡A and is endplayed. If he exits with a club, your hand will be high. If instead he plays a red card, you will ruff in dummy and discard the ♣Q from your hand.

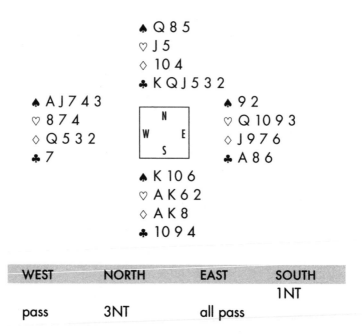

```
              ♠ Q 8 5
              ♡ J 5
              ◊ 10 4
              ♣ K Q J 5 3 2
♠ A J 7 4 3              ♠ 9 2
♡ 8 7 4        N         ♡ Q 10 9 3
◊ Q 5 3 2    W   E       ◊ J 9 7 6
♣ 7            S         ♣ A 8 6
              ♠ K 10 6
              ♡ A K 6 2
              ◊ A K 8
              ♣ 10 9 4
```

WEST	NORTH	EAST	SOUTH
			1NT
pass	3NT	all pass	

Not fancying an eleven-trick game with only 9 points and no singleton in his hand, North declines to mention his clubs and raises to 3NT. West leads the ♠4 to East's ♠9. What is your plan for the contract?

The original declarer displayed his expertise by playing the deal very quickly indeed. He won with the ♠10 and played a club to the king, which was allowed to win. East help up his ace on the next round of clubs too and the contract could no longer be made. When clubs were cleared, East played his remaining spade through South's ♠K-6. South tried his luck with the spade king but West held up his ace to kill the spade entry to dummy. Declarer had only two tricks in each suit for a total of eight. Down one! He had played with impressive speed but insufficient skill.

It is almost certain that West holds the ♠A. (Indeed, if his ♠4 is a true fourth-best card the Rule of Eleven tells you that he does hold the spade ace.) You should therefore win the opening lead with the ♠K, an unnecessarily high card. East refuses to part with his ♣A until the third round, as before. Whatever the defenders do next, you will be able to reach dummy with the ♠Q. Retaining the ♠K at Trick 1 prevents you using from using the spade queen as an entry. You would have to make exactly the same play, winning with the ♠K, if you held K-J-x in the suit.

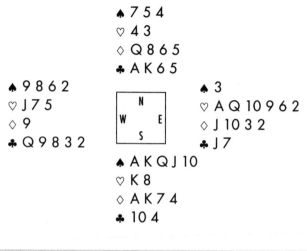

♠ 7 5 4
♡ 4 3
◇ Q 8 6 5
♣ A K 6 5

♠ 9 8 6 2
♡ J 7 5
◇ 9
♣ Q 9 8 3 2

♠ 3
♡ A Q 10 9 6 2
◇ J 10 3 2
♣ J 7

♠ A K Q J 10
♡ K 8
◇ A K 7 4
♣ 10 4

WEST	NORTH	EAST	SOUTH
		2♡*	dbl
pass	3♣*	pass	3♠
pass	4♠	pass	4NT
pass	5♣*	pass	6♠
all pass			

North-South were playing Lebensohl responses to a double of a weak two-bid. North's 3♣ response therefore suggested about 8-10 points. Playing 1430 responses to RKCB, his 5♣ bid showed 1 or 4 keycards. How would you play 6♠ when West leads the ◇9?

Your first task is to read the opening lead. It is surely a singleton since West would have led his partner's suit otherwise. You must therefore win the opening lead with dummy's ◇Q, retaining the ace and king of diamonds over East's jack-ten. Is that an end to the matter? No, because later in the play you will need to make three plays from dummy — two to pick up the diamonds and one to lead towards the ♡K. This will be possible only if you unblock the ◇7 on the first trick!

Having performed such heroics at Trick 1, you draw trumps in four rounds and throw a heart (or a club) from dummy. You cross to the dummy with a club and lead the ◇8. If East plays low, you will run the card successfully and subsequently lead towards the ♡K. Suppose instead that East covers with the ◇10. You win and return to dummy with the ♣K. You can then lead the ◇6. If East covers again, with the ◇J, you can overtake the ◇4 with the ◇5 and lead a heart up to the king.

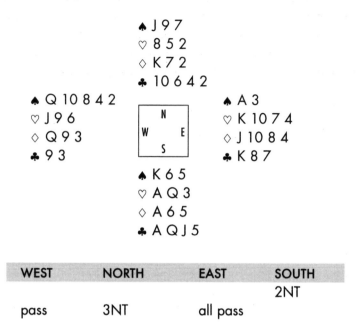

♠ J 9 7
♡ 8 5 2
◇ K 7 2
♣ 10 6 4 2

♠ Q 10 8 4 2
♡ J 9 6
◇ Q 9 3
♣ 9 3

♠ A 3
♡ K 10 7 4
◇ J 10 8 4
♣ K 8 7

♠ K 6 5
♡ A Q 3
◇ A 6 5
♣ A Q J 5

WEST	NORTH	EAST	SOUTH
			2NT
pass	3NT	all pass	

West leads the ♠4 against your contract of 3NT and East wins with the spade ace. As is to be expected, with 20 points opposite 4, the contract is not a brilliant one. You will need four club tricks and two heart tricks to go with your three winners in spades and diamonds.

Dummy is short of entries and you will aid your cause if you drop the ♠K under East's ♠A. The purpose of this move is to promote dummy's ♠J into an entry. The defenders cannot beat the contract now. Let's suppose that East returns the ♠3, West winning with the queen and returning a spade to dummy's jack.

There is no need to lead the ♣10 (which might be costly if East held a singleton ♣K). Lead a low club to the queen, winning the trick. Return to dummy with the ◇K and play a club to the jack, both defenders following. The ace of clubs will now drop East's king and you can return to dummy with a club to the ten to take the heart finesse. With the cards lying in such a friendly fashion, the game is yours.

Suppose East had switched to a diamond instead. The play would be very similar. You would win with the ◇ K and play a low club to the queen. Then you would lead a spade, setting up an extra entry to dummy. When you eventually reached dummy with a spade, you would repeat the club finesse. As before you could then reach dummy with the ♣ 10 on the fourth round of the suit and finesse in hearts.

Problem 13

```
        ♠ 5
        ♡ A J 9 6 2
        ◇ A 7
        ♣ A 10 9 7 6
◇K led

        ♠ A K Q J 10 7 3
        ♡ 4
        ◇ J 5 4
        ♣ K 4
```

WEST	NORTH	EAST	SOUTH
			1♠
pass	2♡	pass	4♠
pass	6♠	all pass	

West leads the ◇K against your spade slam. How will you play?

Problem 14

```
        ♠ J 2
        ♡ A Q 4 3
        ◇ 6 2
        ♣ A K J 8 3
♠K led

        ♠ A 7 4 3
        ♡ K 9 8 6 5 2
        ◇ K Q 3
        ♣ —
```

WEST	NORTH	EAST	SOUTH
	1♣	pass	1♡
1♠	3♡	pass	6♡
all pass			

West leads the ♠K against 6♡. How will you play the contract?

Problem 15 ··

♠ Q 10 6
♡ A J 10 9 8 4
◇ 5 3
♣ K 4

♠8 led

♠ A J 4
♡ K
◇ A K 9 2
♣ J 8 7 3 2

WEST	NORTH	EAST	SOUTH
		1♠	pass
pass	2♡	pass	3NT
all pass			

West leads the ♠8 against 3NT. How will you play?

Problem 16 ··

♠ A 6
♡ J 4 2
◇ K 9 6 5 2
♣ K 7 3

♣Q led

♠ K Q J 10 9 7
♡ A 5
◇ A 3
♣ A 8 5

WEST	NORTH	EAST	SOUTH
			1♠
pass	2◇	pass	3♠
pass	4♠	pass	6♠
all pass			

West leads the ♣Q against your small slam in spades. How will you plan the play?

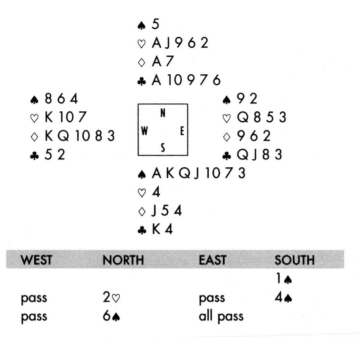

```
                    ♠ 5
                    ♡ A J 9 6 2
                    ◇ A 7
                    ♣ A 10 9 7 6
♠ 8 6 4                              ♠ 9 2
♡ K 10 7            N                ♡ Q 8 5 3
◇ K Q 10 8 3   W        E            ◇ 9 6 2
♣ 5 2                  S             ♣ Q J 8 3
                    ♠ A K Q J 10 7 3
                    ♡ 4
                    ◇ J 5 4
                    ♣ K 4
```

WEST	NORTH	EAST	SOUTH
			1♠
pass	2♡	pass	4♠
pass	6♠	all pass	

West leads the ◇K against your spade slam. You have two potential losers in the diamond suit and must reduce these to one. If the defenders permit it, you may be able to ruff the third round of diamonds with dummy's singleton trump. Otherwise you will have to set up a long club for a diamond discard.

Suppose you win the first round of diamonds. This will kill both your intended lines of play. If you continue with another round of diamonds, the defenders will win and remove dummy's trump. With the clubs breaking 4-2, you will not have enough entries to switch plans and establish the club suit.

Instead you should duck the first round of diamonds. What can West do? He can prevent a diamond ruff by switching to trumps, but the ◇A will remain as an entry. You will then be able to draw trumps and establish a long club with two ruffs, finally returning to dummy with the remaining red ace to discard a diamond on the long club. If instead West persists with diamonds, to remove the entry, you will score a diamond ruff instead.

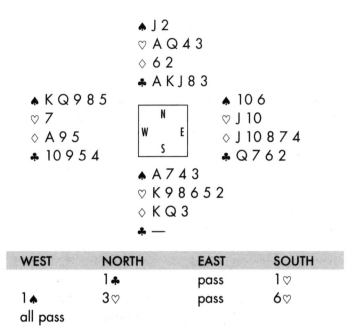

WEST	NORTH	EAST	SOUTH
	1♣	pass	1♡
1♠	3♡	pass	6♡
all pass			

West leads the ♠K against your small slam in hearts. It's an ambitious contract and prospects are not awe-inspiring. How will you play it?

You must try to set up dummy's clubs. If the defenders' clubs break 4-4 or the ♣Q falls in three rounds, you will be able to throw all three spade losers from the South hand. Entries to dummy are at a premium, so you must remember to keep your ♡2, so that you can use this to cross to the table later.

You win the spade lead with the ace and lead the ♡5 to dummy's ♡A, both defenders following. You then ruff a club with the ♡6 and return to dummy by leading the ♡8 to the ♡Q. Both defenders follow to the ace and king of clubs. You discard two spade losers from your hand and ruff a club with the ♡9. Yes! The clubs break 4-4. All that remains is to tidy up the loose ends. You cross to dummy by leading the ♡2 to the ♡3, impressing everyone present. You then discard your last spade loser on the established club and ruff a spade in your hand. The final task is to lead the ◊K, dislodging the ace. After scoring the ◊Q, you will ruff your last diamond in the dummy.

$\spadesuit$ Q 10 6
$\heartsuit$ A J 10 9 8 4
$\diamondsuit$ 5 3
$\clubsuit$ K 4

$\spadesuit$ 8 5 $\spadesuit$ K 9 7 3 2
$\heartsuit$ Q 7 3 2 $\heartsuit$ 6 5
$\diamondsuit$ 10 7 6 4 $\diamondsuit$ Q J 8
$\clubsuit$ 10 9 5 $\clubsuit$ A Q 6

$\spadesuit$ A J 4
$\heartsuit$ K
$\diamondsuit$ A K 9 2
$\clubsuit$ J 8 7 3 2

WEST	NORTH	EAST	SOUTH
		1$\spadesuit$	pass
pass	2$\heartsuit$	pass	3NT
all pass			

Perhaps you should have found your way to 4$\heartsuit$ but you end in the more difficult contract of 3NT. West leads the $\spadesuit$8. What is your plan?

You must aim to set up partner's heart suit and entries to the dummy are in short supply. The contract cannot be made, in fact, unless you combine two clever entry-creating plays. The first is to play the $\spadesuit$6 from the dummy and to win West's $\spadesuit$8 with the ace rather than the jack. By doing so, you ensure that you can later cross to dummy in the spade suit. The next clever move comes immediately — you must overtake the king of hearts with dummy's ace. You then drive out the $\heartsuit$Q, setting up a total of five heart tricks.

There is nothing West can do. Let's suppose he plays a diamond to the jack and your ace. You play a spade to the ten and, whether or not East wins the trick, you will eventually gain access to the dummy. You will score two spades (having surrendered one trick in that suit), five hearts and the diamond ace-king.

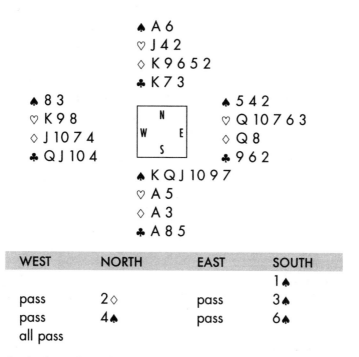

	♠ A 6	
	♡ J 4 2	
	◊ K 9 6 5 2	
	♣ K 7 3	

♠ 8 3	N	♠ 5 4 2
♡ K 9 8	W E	♡ Q 10 7 6 3
◊ J 10 7 4	S	◊ Q 8
♣ Q J 10 4		♣ 9 6 2

	♠ K Q J 10 9 7	
	♡ A 5	
	◊ A 3	
	♣ A 8 5	

WEST	NORTH	EAST	SOUTH
			1♠
pass	2◊	pass	3♠
pass	4♠	pass	6♠
all pass			

West leads the ♣Q against your small slam in spades. You have two potential losers, one in hearts and one in clubs, and the only sensible chance of disposing of one (or both) of them is to set up dummy's diamond suit. Since entries to dummy will be valuable in achieving this, you should win the club lead in the South hand, with the ace.

Suppose you draw three rounds of trumps next, wasting dummy's ♠A as an entry. You can play the ace and king of diamonds, followed by a diamond ruff, but unless diamonds break 3-3 you will go down. A better idea is to draw only one round of trumps with the king. You then play the ace and king of diamonds and ruff a third round of diamonds (ruffing high if East follows suit). The suit breaks 4-2 but you now have two entries left to the dummy. You cross to the ♠A and ruff another diamond, setting up a long card in the suit. After drawing East's last trump, you can return to dummy with the ♣K to discard one of your losers on the thirteenth diamond. Slam made!

Problem 17

```
                    ♠ 3
                    ♡ A Q
                    ◇ A J 8 4 3
                    ♣ A J 7 3 2
    ♣ 10 led

                    ♠ A K Q J 10 8
                    ♡ J 10 9 8 3
                    ◇ 7
                    ♣ 6
```

WEST	NORTH	EAST	SOUTH
			1♠
pass	2◇	pass	2♡
pass	3♣ *	pass	4♡
pass	6♡	pass	6♠
all pass			

How will you play 6♠ when West leads the ♣10?

Problem 18

```
                    ♠ 8 5 2
                    ♡ J 6 4
                    ◇ 10 9 7
                    ♣ A Q 10 3
    ♡ 10 led

                    ♠ A Q J
                    ♡ A K Q
                    ◇ A J 4
                    ♣ K J 5 2
```

WEST	NORTH	EAST	SOUTH
			2♣
pass	2◇	pass	3NT
pass	6NT	all pass	

West leads the ♡10 against your slam. What is your plan?

Problem 19 ·····························

```
              ♠ K J 7 6 4
              ♡ 6
              ◇ 10 4 3
              ♣ Q 9 8 2
  ◇K led
              ♠ A
              ♡ A K Q J 10 5 3 2
              ◇ A 6
              ♣ A 7
```

WEST	NORTH	EAST	SOUTH
3◇	pass	pass	6♡
all pass			

West leads the ◇K against your slam, East following with the ◇2. How will you play the contract?

Problem 20 ·····························

```
              ♠ 10 6
              ♡ J 5
              ◇ A K Q 10 6
              ♣ A K J 6
  ♡3 led
              ♠ K Q J 9 5 4
              ♡ 10 8 2
              ◇ J 7 5
              ♣ 8
```

WEST	NORTH	EAST	SOUTH
		1♡	2♠
pass	4♠	all pass	

West leads the ♡3 to East's ace and the ◇3 is returned. How do you read the situation? What can you do about it?

```
                    ♠ 3
                    ♡ A Q
                    ◇ A J 8 4 3
                    ♣ A J 7 3 2
  ♠ 4                                  ♠ 9 7 6 5 2
  ♡ K 7 6 2          ┌─────────┐       ♡ 5 4
  ◇ Q 10 9 6 2       │    N    │       ◇ K 5
  ♣ 10 9 5           │ W     E │       ♣ K Q 8 4
                     │    S    │
                     └─────────┘
                    ♠ A K Q J 10 8
                    ♡ J 10 9 8 3
                    ◇ 7
                    ♣ 6
```

WEST	NORTH	EAST	SOUTH
			1♠
pass	2◇	pass	2♡
pass	3♣ *	pass	4♡
pass	6♡	pass	6♠
all pass			

A somewhat unpolished auction carries you to 6♠. How will you play this contract when West leads the ♣10?

Suppose you win with the ♣A and draw trumps in five rounds. You will then go down against best defense. If you subsequently play the ace and queen of hearts, West will hold up the king. You would have to ruff with your last trump to reach your hand again and, with no further entry to your hand available, there would then be no point in setting up the hearts.

How about playing the ace and queen of hearts before drawing trumps? That's no good. West will win and play a third heart, allowing his partner to overruff the dummy.

As the cards lie, it is good enough to draw trumps, discarding the ♡A and ♡Q from dummy. You can then lead the ♡J to force out the ♡K, claiming the balance. If the hearts divided 5-1, this line would fail. You would lose a trick on the fifth round of the suit. So, the very best play is to cash the ♡A before drawing trumps. You can then discard the ♡Q on the second round of trumps and be absolutely certain to score three further heart tricks with your ♡J-10-9-8.

♠ 8 5 2
♡ J 6 4
◇ 10 9 7
♣ A Q 10 3

♠ 7 6 4
♡ 10 9 8 2
◇ Q 6 5
♣ 9 8 4

```
     N
  W     E
     S
```

♠ K 10 9 3
♡ 7 5 3
◇ K 8 3 2
♣ 7 6

♠ A Q J
♡ A K Q
◇ A J 4
♣ K J 5 2

WEST	NORTH	EAST	SOUTH
			2♣
pass	2◇	pass	3NT
pass	6NT	all pass	

West leads the ♡10 and you win in the South hand, noting that you will need some luck to land the contract. East must hold the ♠K and at least one of the missing diamond honors. Meanwhile, you may need four entries to dummy to take the required finesses in spades and diamonds. How can you manage that?

At Trick 2 you should lead the ♣K to dummy's ♣A. By disposing of your king in this way, you promote the value of dummy's remaining cards in the suit. Both defenders follow suit and you finesse the ♠Q successfully. Next you lead the ♣5 to dummy's ♣10, pleased to see that the clubs break 3-2. You repeat the spade finesse successfully and prospects now look good.

You re-enter dummy by leading the ♣J to the ♣Q. When you run the ◇10, West wins with the queen and exits safely with a spade to your ace. You then lead the ♣2 to the ♣3 to take a second diamond finesse.

This wins and the slam is yours. (You can transpose the first two rounds of clubs, starting with the ♣5 to the ♣10.)

When clubs break 4-1, you cannot overtake afford to overtake on the third round. With only three entries available to dummy, you would then need East to hold both diamond honors or a singleton or doubleton diamond honor. In both those cases one diamond lead from dummy would be sufficient to set up a second diamond trick.

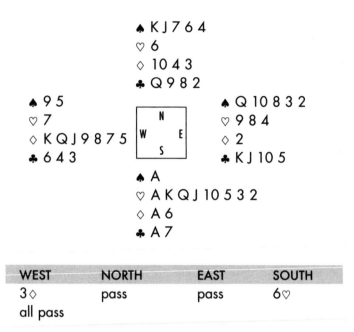

WEST	NORTH	EAST	SOUTH
3◇	pass	pass	6♡
all pass			

West's diamond preempt runs to you in the South seat. How can you tell if your partner holds the precious ♣K? You decide to invoke an age-old technique — you will bid the slam and find out about the ♣K when dummy comes down! West leads the ◇K and dummy appears with the wrong black king. How will you play the slam?

East's ◇2 confirms that diamonds are breaking 7-1. If East holds three trumps and the ♣K, both of which are quite likely, you will be able to endplay him. You win the diamond lead and play the ace and king of trumps, West showing out on the second round. You play the ♠A and then lead the two of trumps, throwing East in. Like it or not, he must now give you an entry to dummy. You have sacrificed one trick in trumps but you will gain two tricks in return. If East exits with a spade, you will score the jack and king of the suit, allowing you to throw your two minor-suit losers. If East plays a club instead, this will spare you a club loser and you can throw your remaining diamond on the king of spades.

Why did we say it was quite likely that East held three trumps? A preemptor usually holds a singleton somewhere. When it is a side-suit singleton, he will often lead it. West's actual diamond lead suggested that his singleton would be in the trump suit. Also, of course, he is more likely to have a singleton in a suit where you hold nine cards between the combined hands than in one where you hold six cards.

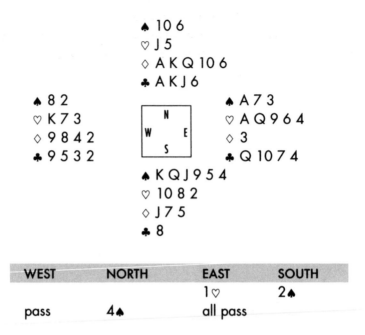

WEST	NORTH	EAST	SOUTH
		1♡	2♠
pass	4♠	all pass	

Partner raises your weak jump overcall to game and West leads the ♡3 to East's ace. How will you play when East returns the ◇3?

It is not difficult to read the situation. East surely holds a singleton diamond and is hoping for a diamond ruff. Suppose you simply win the diamond switch and play a trump. East will win with the trump ace and cross to the West hand with a heart to the king. (East's play of the ♡A at Trick 1 tells you that West holds the ♡K.) A diamond ruff will then sink the contract. The question is: what can you do about it?

The path to the West hand is in hearts and you must aim to destroy this line of communication. Play the ace and king of clubs, throwing one of your hearts. Then play the jack of clubs, throwing your last heart. East has to win the trick (no surprise, since his opening bid marks him with the ♣Q) and the safe hand is left on lead. Since there is no route to the West hand, the defenders cannot score a diamond ruff and you will make the contract. The 'entry management' on this deal involved the *defenders'* entries, which you managed to their disadvantage!

Look again at what happened. You swapped a heart loser for a club loser. This helped your cause because West could have won the second round of hearts whereas only East could capture the ♣J.

Problem 21

　　　　　　　　♠ Q 6 3
　　　　　　　　♡ 9 7 6
　　　　　　　　◇ 10 6 3
　　　　　　　　♣ A J 10 5

◇K led

　　　　　　　　♠ K 7 5
　　　　　　　　♡ A K Q 10 4 3
　　　　　　　　◇ A
　　　　　　　　♣ 9 6 2

WEST	NORTH	EAST	SOUTH
			1♡
1♠	2♡	pass	4♡
all pass			

West leads the ◇K against your game in hearts. How will you plan the play? (Trumps are not 4-0.)

Problem 22

　　　　　　　　♠ A 9 6
　　　　　　　　♡ 10 6 2
　　　　　　　　◇ J 7
　　　　　　　　♣ A 6 5 3 2

♠K led

　　　　　　　　♠ 8 4
　　　　　　　　♡ A K 4
　　　　　　　　◇ A 10 5 3
　　　　　　　　♣ K Q 9 7

WEST	NORTH	EAST	SOUTH
			1NT
3♠	3NT	all pass	

West leads the ♠K against your contract of 3NT. Do you foresee any problems? How will you play?

Problem 23

```
              ♠ J 9 8
              ♡ A 9 7 3
              ♦ J 8 4
              ♣ 7 5 2
  ♡Q led
              ♠ A K Q 10 3
              ♡ 6
              ♦ A K Q 7
              ♣ A K 6
```

WEST	NORTH	EAST	SOUTH
			2♣
pass	2♦	pass	2♠
pass	3♠	pass	4NT
pass	5♣*	pass	7♠
all pass			

West leads the ♡Q against your (somewhat wildly bid) grand slam. How will you play?

Problem 24

```
              ♠ A Q J 4
              ♡ —
              ♦ A K Q 9 7 2
              ♣ A 7 4
  ♡K led
              ♠ K 9 7 2
              ♡ 10 5
              ♦ 8 6 5 3
              ♣ 10 6 3
```

WEST	NORTH	EAST	SOUTH
4♡	dbl	pass	4♠
pass	6♠	all pass	

West leads the ♡K against your spade slam. How do you plan to make twelve tricks?

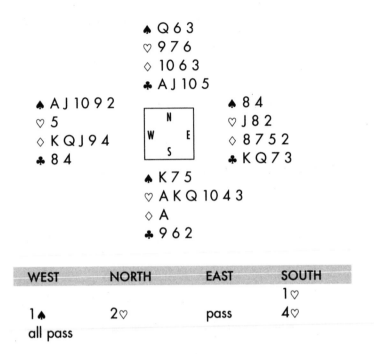

♠ Q 6 3
♡ 9 7 6
◇ 10 6 3
♣ A J 10 5

♠ A J 10 9 2
♡ 5
◇ K Q J 9 4
♣ 8 4

♠ 8 4
♡ J 8 2
◇ 8 7 5 2
♣ K Q 7 3

♠ K 7 5
♡ A K Q 10 4 3
◇ A
♣ 9 6 2

WEST	NORTH	EAST	SOUTH
			1♡
1♠	2♡	pass	4♡
all pass			

West leads the ◇K against your heart game and you win with the bare ace. A trump loser is unlikely but this still leaves you with two potential losers in each black suit. In clubs you can take a double finesse. Even if both finesses lose, you will be left with a spare club winner that can be used for discarding a spade. The problem is: how can you stop the defenders cashing two spade tricks before you can take a discard on the long club?

You should draw trumps in three rounds and lead the ♣9. If West covers with an honor, your problems are over. You will win with the ace and clear a second club trick. That will give you a total of six hearts, one spade, two clubs and a diamond. When the cards lie as in the diagram, the ♣9 will run to East's queen (or king). He returns the ♠8 and the key point of the deal has been reached. If you play low from your hand on this trick, West will also play low and dummy's ♠Q will be forced. When the second club finesse also loses, East will play a spade through your K-x and you will lose two spades, going down one.

To break the defenders' communications, you must rise with the king on the first round of spades. West cannot duck or you will score two spade tricks. If he takes the ace and returns a spade, East will have no spade to play when the next club finesse loses.

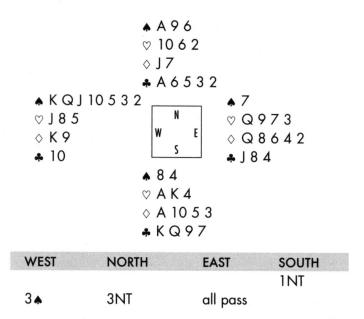

♠ A 9 6
♡ 10 6 2
◇ J 7
♣ A 6 5 3 2

♠ K Q J 10 5 3 2
♡ J 8 5
◇ K 9
♣ 10

♠ 7
♡ Q 9 7 3
◇ Q 8 6 4 2
♣ J 8 4

♠ 8 4
♡ A K 4
◇ A 10 5 3
♣ K Q 9 7

WEST	NORTH	EAST	SOUTH
			1NT
3♠	3NT	all pass	

West leads the ♠K against 3NT. On a cursory glance it may seem that nine tricks are cold unless the clubs break 4-0. Look again! Even a 3-1 club break will cause a problem because all four spot-cards in the dummy are lower than the two in your hand. This means that you will be forced to win the fourth round of clubs in the South hand and cannot reach the last club in dummy. What can be done?

The solution is to duck the first two rounds of spades, even though the bidding tells you East cannot hold more than two spades. Your intention is to throw the ♣9 or ♣7 on dummy's ace of spades. After this clever move you will have no problem in scoring five club tricks (unless clubs break 4-0).

Suppose that West is a genius and diagnoses your problem, switching to a heart or a club at Trick 2. You will match him for cleverness by winning his switch and ducking a second round of spades yourself. Whatever he tries next, you will be able to play the king, queen and ace of clubs. You can then discard your troublesome last club on the ♠A.

```
                    ♠ J 9 8
                    ♡ A 9 7 3
                    ◇ J 8 4
                    ♣ 7 5 2
    ♠ 6 4                           ♠ 7 5 2
    ♡ Q J 10 4        ┌─────┐       ♡ K 8 5 2
    ◇ 10 6 2          │  N  │       ◇ 9 5 3
    ♣ Q 10 9 3     W  │     │  E    ♣ J 8 4
                      │  S  │
                      └─────┘
                    ♠ A K Q 10 3
                    ♡ 6
                    ◇ A K Q 7
                    ♣ A K 6
```

WEST	NORTH	EAST	SOUTH
			2♣
pass	2◇	pass	2♠
pass	3♠	pass	4NT
pass	5♣*	pass	7♠
all pass			

South had no reason to expect his minor-suit losers to vanish into thin air but he leapt to 7♠ nevertheless. 'I like to enjoy my bridge,' he explained afterwards. How would you play the grand slam when West leads the ♡Q?

If you study the loser situation from the South hand, the situation is unattractive. Dummy's ◇J has rescued you in diamonds but what can you do with the club loser? Next view the deal from the North seat. North has three heart losers, all of which can be ruffed in the South hand, and one club loser that can be discarded on the fourth round of diamonds. That looks better! By playing a dummy reversal, ruffing three hearts in the long-trump hand, it seems that thirteen tricks will materialize.

How does the play go? You win the heart lead and ruff a heart with the ♠A, retaining your lower trumps so that you can cross to dummy later. Cross to the ◇J and ruff another heart with the ♠K. The way is now clear for you to lead the ♠3 to dummy's ♠8. A third heart ruff with the ♠Q allows you to lead your ♠10 to dummy's ♠J. On this trick you are praying that the trumps will divide 3-2. Yes, the suit behaves honorably. You draw East's last trump and claim the remaining tricks. The grand slam is yours.

You remember the old-timer's adage: always lead a trump against a grand slam? If West had followed this advice, there would have been no way to make the contract!

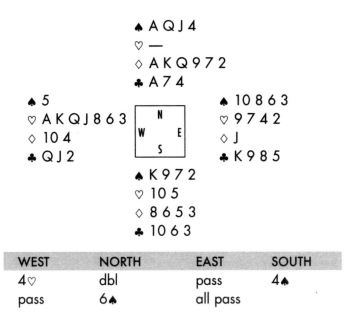

♠ A Q J 4
♡ —
◇ A K Q 9 7 2
♣ A 7 4

♠ 5
♡ A K Q J 8 6 3
◇ 10 4
♣ Q J 2

♠ 10 8 6 3
♡ 9 7 4 2
◇ J
♣ K 9 8 5

♠ K 9 7 2
♡ 10 5
◇ 8 6 5 3
♣ 10 6 3

WEST	NORTH	EAST	SOUTH
4♡	dbl	pass	4♠
pass	6♠	all pass	

West leads the ♡K against your spade slam. You ruff in dummy with the ♠4 and... Do you? If so, you will go down. After cashing the ace, queen and jack of trumps, there will be no entry to the South hand to draw the last trump. Nor will turning to the diamond suit do you any good. East will ruff the second diamond and the defenders will score a heart trick.

So that you can overcome ♠10-x-x-x with East, you should make the spectacular play of ruffing the opening heart lead with dummy's ♠A! When the queen and jack of trumps reveal the situation you can lead the precious ♠4 for a finesse of the ♠9. You then draw East's last trump and end with four trump tricks, six diamond tricks, the ♣A and one heart ruff. Twelve of the best. Nothing can be lost by ruffing high on the first trick. If West started with ♠10-x-x-x, you could not make the slam anyway.

Before you turn the page, note what a good idea of yours it was to remove partner's double of 4♡. Such a double nearly always contains preparedness to play in spades. If you had passed the double for penalties, the heart game would have been made!

Problem 25

```
        ♠ 6
        ♡ Q 9 5
        ◇ A J 7
        ♣ A J 10 9 7 3
◇ 2 led

        ♠ A 8 4 2
        ♡ K 6
        ◇ K Q 10 9 6 5
        ♣ 4
```

WEST	NORTH	EAST	SOUTH
			1◇
pass	2♣	pass	2◇
pass	3♠*	pass	4NT
pass	5♡*	pass	6◇
all pass			

How will you play 6◇ when West leads a trump?

Problem 26

```
        ♠ J 6
        ♡ 9 8 7 5 2
        ◇ Q 8 5
        ♣ K 7 4
◇ J led

        ♠ A Q 9 8 5 4 2
        ♡ A K 10
        ◇ A K
        ♣ A
```

WEST	NORTH	EAST	SOUTH
			2♣
pass	2◇	pass	2♠
pass	2NT	pass	3♠
pass	4♣	pass	6♠
all pass			

West leads the ◇J against your spade slam. How will you play?

Problem 27

```
            ♠ A Q 10
            ♡ 8 3 2
            ◇ 9 7 5 4 3
            ♣ J 4
  ♣10 led
            ♠ K 5 3
            ♡ A K 7
            ◇ A K J 8
            ♣ A K 2
```

WEST	NORTH	EAST	SOUTH
			2♣
pass	2◇	pass	3NT
pass	6NT	all pass	

West leads the ♣10 against 6NT. Without much hope you call for
dummy's ♣J, covered by the queen and ace. When you cash the ◇A
West shows out. How will you continue?

Problem 28

```
            ♠ K Q 3
            ♡ 10 4
            ◇ A K 9 7 4 2
            ♣ 9 4
  ♣Q led
            ♠ A 9 7 6 4 2
            ♡ A 7 6 5 3
            ◇ 5
            ♣ A
```

WEST	NORTH	EAST	SOUTH
	1◇	pass	1♠
pass	2◇	pass	2♡
pass	3♠	pass	4NT
pass	5♠*	pass	6♠
all pass			

Only 24 points between the hands, yes, but it is a good slam. How will
you plan the play when West leads the ♣Q?

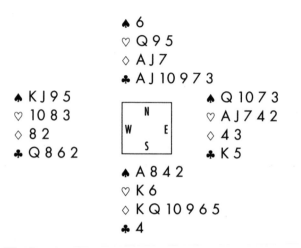

♠ 6
♡ Q 9 5
◇ A J 7
♣ A J 10 9 7 3

♠ K J 9 5
♡ 10 8 3
◇ 8 2
♣ Q 8 6 2

♠ Q 10 7 3
♡ A J 7 4 2
◇ 4 3
♣ K 5

♠ A 8 4 2
♡ K 6
◇ K Q 10 9 6 5
♣ 4

WEST	NORTH	EAST	SOUTH
			1◇
pass	2♣	pass	2◇
pass	3♠*	pass	4NT
pass	5♡*	pass	6◇
all pass			

West leads a low trump against your small slam in diamonds. How will you plan the play?

You have a certain heart loser and, after the opening trump lead, will not be able to ruff all three losing spades. You must therefore aim to set up dummy's club suit. After winning the trump lead, you play the ace of clubs and ruff a club, the king appearing from East. You then make the key move — leading the ♡K from your hand.

East has two losing options. Let's suppose first that he wins with the ♡A and returns another trump. This removes an entry to dummy but the ♡Q will now serve as an extra entry. You win the second trump in dummy and ruff a club. You then cross to dummy with the ♡Q and ruff another club, setting up the suit. Finally you reach dummy with a spade ruff and throw two spades on the established clubs.

Now let's see what happens if East holds up the ♡A with the intention of depriving you of an extra entry to dummy. You cross to dummy with a second round of trumps and lead the ♣J, discarding your remaining heart! The club suit is now established and you have exchanged your losing heart for a losing club. You can win West's return and enter dummy with a spade ruff to discard your remaining spade losers on dummy's club winners.

The play follows a similar path when West holds ♣K-x or ♣Q-x. You will also make the contract easily when clubs break 3-3. When West holds ♣K-Q-x-x, you can succeed only by a double-dummy play. You would have to cross to the ♠A and lead a club towards dummy, intending to finesse the ♣J if West played low.

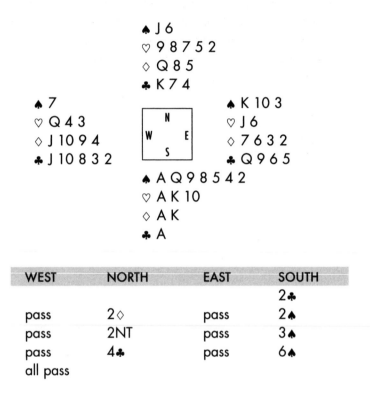

	♠ J 6		
	♡ 9 8 7 5 2		
	◇ Q 8 5		
	♣ K 7 4		

WEST	NORTH	EAST	SOUTH
			2♣
pass	2◇	pass	2♠
pass	2NT	pass	3♠
pass	4♣	pass	6♠
all pass			

North's 4♣ was a cuebid with spades agreed. How would you play the small slam in spades when West leads the ◇J?

You win the diamond lead and cash the ♣A. If you can reach dummy, you will be able to throw your potential heart loser on the ♣K. One possibility is simply to lead a low spade towards the jack. If West holds the ♠K you will be able to reach dummy. That is only a 50% chance, though.

You can give yourself a better chance by leading the ♠Q from your hand. If a defender wins with the ♠K, dummy's ♠J will become an entry. The defenders will have no choice in the matter, obviously, when the ♠K is singleton. When the king is doubleton, they can hold it up only at the expense of having it dropped by the ace on the second round. What will happen when a defender has ♠K-x-x and refuses to win the queen? In that case you are not necessarily dead! When the cards lie as in the diagram, East ducks your ♠Q and West shows out on the ♠A. Now you cash your other diamond winner and the top hearts. You exit with a trump to the king and East has no heart to play! He is endplayed — forced to give you an entry to dummy.

```
                    ♠ A Q 10
                    ♡ 8 3 2
                    ◇ 9 7 5 4 3
                    ♣ J 4
   ♠ J 9 8 7 4                        ♠ 6 2
   ♡ Q 10 6         ┌─────────┐       ♡ J 9 5 4
   ◇ —             │    N    │        ◇ Q 10 6 2
   ♣ 10 9 8 7 5     │ W     E │       ♣ Q 6 3
                    │    S    │
                    └─────────┘
                    ♠ K 5 3
                    ♡ A K 7
                    ◇ A K J 8
                    ♣ A K 2
```

WEST	NORTH	EAST	SOUTH
			2♣
pass	2◇	pass	3NT
pass	6NT	all pass	

Hoping that his diamond suit will have a role to play, North raises you to 6NT. West leads the ♣10 and, whether or not you bother to commit dummy's ♣J, you win the first trick in your hand. When you cash the ◇A, West shows out. What now?

To score the five diamond tricks that you need, you will have to enter dummy three times — twice to take diamond finesses and once more to score the long diamond. In theory you could conjure three entries in the spade suit by dropping a doubleton ♠J from East and leading a low spade to the 10 on the third round. It is a much better chance, obviously, to finesse West for the ♠J.

At Trick 3 you play the ♠K to dummy's ♠A, just in case East has a singleton ♠J. You then finesse the ◇8 (East would cover if you tried the ◇9 instead). Now you must steel yourself for a spade finesse that would be unnecessary if you did not need to create an extra entry to dummy. A spade to the 10 wins! You finesse the ◇J, cash the ◇K and re-enter dummy with the ♠Q to score the long diamond. By a combination of luck and skill you have scored twelve tricks.

(Note that it is not as good to play low to the ♠Q on the first round. If you subsequently led your remaining low card, intending to finesse dummy's ♠10, West could thwart you by inserting the ♠J. You would have to win with the ace, restricting yourself to only two entries.)

SOLUTION TO PROBLEM 28

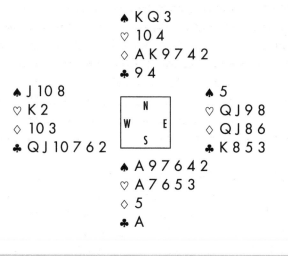

♠ K Q 3
♡ 10 4
◇ A K 9 7 4 2
♣ 9 4

♠ J 10 8
♡ K 2
◇ 10 3
♣ Q J 10 7 6 2

♠ 5
♡ Q J 9 8
◇ Q J 8 6
♣ K 8 5 3

♠ A 9 7 6 4 2
♡ A 7 6 5 3
◇ 5
♣ A

WEST	NORTH	EAST	SOUTH
	1◇	pass	1♠
pass	2◇	pass	2♡
pass	3♠	pass	4NT
pass	5♠*	pass	6♠
all pass			

West leads the ♣Q against 6♠. You have four losing cards in hearts and can afford to concede only one trick there. To achieve this, you must establish one of the red suits. If you play to set up the hearts, ruffing in dummy, your chances will be slim unless the suit breaks 3-3. A much better prospect is to establish dummy's diamonds, which can be done when the diamonds break no worse than 4-2.

You must play diamonds before drawing trumps, since you will eventually need a trump entry to reach the established diamonds. Let's see what happens if you win the club lead, cross to the ◇A and ruff a diamond. When you play the ace and king of trumps, the suit fails to break 2-2. You ruff another diamond because you will still make the slam if diamonds are 3-3 or if West started with four diamonds. Unfortunately West overruffs the third diamond and you are down one.

To set up the diamonds safely, even when West has a doubleton, an unusual move is required. You must duck the first round of diamonds! This will allow you to set up the suit by ruffing the second round (which cannot be overruffed) rather than the third.

At Trick 2 you should draw one round of trumps with the ace, to check that trumps are not 4-0. When both defenders follow to the first trump, you duck a round of diamonds. East wins and returns a heart to the ace. You cross to the king of trumps and ruff a diamond. Since this is only the second round of the suit, West has to follow. The diamonds are now set up. You cross to dummy with the ♠Q, drawing West's last trump, and discard all four of your losing hearts on the established diamonds.

What would happen if trumps happened to be 4-0? You could still succeed if diamonds broke 3-3. Instead of ducking a diamond, you would cross to the ◊A and ruff a diamond. Returning to dummy with a second round of trumps, you would run good diamonds until the defender ruffed. You could then win his return and cross back to dummy with a third round of trumps, drawing the last trump, to enjoy the remaining diamonds.

Problem 29

```
            ♠ 4 3
            ♡ Q 6 3
            ◇ K Q 10 9 6
            ♣ A 10 3
♣K led
            ♠ A J 8
            ♡ A K J 10 5 2
            ◇ A
            ♣ J 9 2
```

WEST	NORTH	EAST	SOUTH
			1♡
pass	2◇	pass	3♡
pass	4♣	pass	4◇
pass	4♡	pass	6♡
all pass			

How will you play the slam when West leads the ♣K?

Problem 30

```
            ♠ 7 6 4
            ♡ A 10 8
            ◇ 8 6 2
            ♣ J 10 8 7
♠2 led
            ♠ A 9 3
            ♡ K Q 5 2
            ◇ A K 4
            ♣ A 9 6
```

WEST	NORTH	EAST	SOUTH
			2NT
pass	3NT	all pass	

West leads a fourth-best ♠2 against 3NT. How will you play the contract?

Problem 31

♠ 9 5 4 2
♡ Q 10 9
♦ 9 7 6
♣ K 6 4

♣Q led

♠ A K Q J 10 8
♡ A J 4
♦ K 3
♣ 8 5

WEST	NORTH	EAST	SOUTH
			1♠
pass	2♠	pass	4♠
all pass			

You play low from dummy on the first two rounds of clubs and West persists with a third club, covered by the dummy's king and East's ace. How will you continue?

Problem 32

♠ 7 2
♡ A K 4
♦ J 6 4 2
♣ A J 5 2

♦10 led

♠ A Q J 10 8 4
♡ Q J 8 7 2
♦ 5
♣ 4

WEST	NORTH	EAST	SOUTH
			1♠
pass	2♣	pass	2♡
pass	3♦*	pass	3♡
pass	4♡	all pass	

The defenders lead and continue diamonds. Obviously there is no problem unless the ♠K is offside and one of the majors breaks 4-1. What is your plan?

```
                    ♠ 4 3
                    ♡ Q 6 3
                    ◇ K Q 10 9 6
                    ♣ A 10 3
    ♠ K 10 6 2          ┌─────────┐        ♠ Q 9 7 5
    ♡ —                 │    N    │        ♡ 9 8 7 4
    ◇ J 8 7 5 4         │ W     E │        ◇ 3 2
    ♣ K Q 6 4           │    S    │        ♣ 8 7 5
                        └─────────┘
                    ♠ A J 8
                    ♡ A K J 10 5 2
                    ◇ A
                    ♣ J 9 2
```

WEST	NORTH	EAST	SOUTH
			1♡
pass	2◇	pass	3♡
pass	4♣	pass	4◇
pass	4♡	pass	6♡
all pass			

West leads the ♣K against your small slam and an inspection of the dummy reveals that you are in an excellent contract. At such a moment you must consider how to guard against an unlucky lie of the cards.

The original declarer played too quickly. He could count eleven top tricks (six trumps, three diamonds and the black aces). After the opening ♣K lead a twelfth trick could be established in clubs, so what could possibly go wrong?

Declarer soon found out. He won the club lead with the ace, following with a low card from his hand. He then crossed to the ace of trumps, discovering that the trumps were 4-0. It was not possible now to draw trumps before cashing the three diamond winners. Declarer unblocked the ◇A and crossed to the ♡Q. Everyone followed to the

◇K and he discarded one of his spade losers. When he played the ◇Q East ruffed and there was no way to recover.

At Trick 1, you should win with the ♣A and unblock your ♣J. After drawing trumps in four rounds, you cash the ◇A and lead a club towards the ♣10. Nothing can prevent you from reaching dummy to enjoy the two diamond winners.

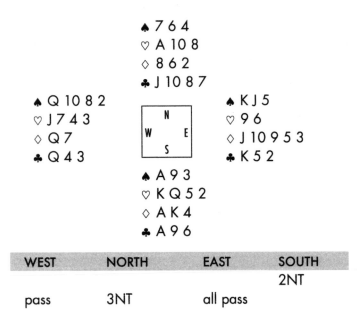

♠ 7 6 4
♡ A 10 8
◇ 8 6 2
♣ J 10 8 7

♠ Q 10 8 2
♡ J 7 4 3
◇ Q 7
♣ Q 4 3

N
W   E
S

♠ K J 5
♡ 9 6
◇ J 10 9 5 3
♣ K 5 2

♠ A 9 3
♡ K Q 5 2
◇ A K 4
♣ A 9 6

WEST	NORTH	EAST	SOUTH
			2NT
pass	3NT	all pass	

West leads a fourth-best ♠2 against 3NT. If West is an upright citizen whose leads can be trusted, you should win the first spade with the ace. You have seven top tricks and must hope to score a fourth trick in hearts, along with an extra trick in one of the minor suits.

The percentage play in hearts, viewing the suit in isolation, is to play the three top honors in the hope that the jack will come down. This is slightly better than finessing the ♡10. However, a successful finesse of the ♡10 will give you a second entry to dummy and you will then be able to take advantage of the best play in clubs — taking two finesses.

This is, in fact, the best combination of plays available. If a finesse of the ♡10 succeeds, you will make the contract unless West holds both club honors. Your chance of success will be around 40%.

Suppose you play hearts from the top instead. If the ♡J falls doubleton, you will be able to take two club finesses. If the hearts divide 3-3, you will have only one entry to dummy and can therefore make only one club lead towards your hand. You will need East to hold both club honors, or a singleton or doubleton club honor. This gives you around 30% total chance — not so good.

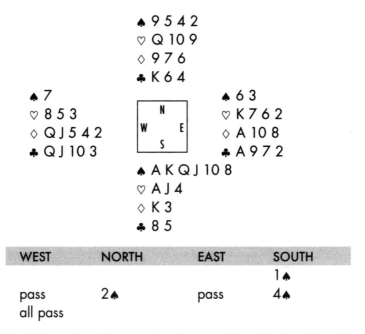

| ♠ 9 5 4 2 |
| ♡ Q 10 9 |
| ◊ 9 7 6 |
| ♣ K 6 4 |

♠ 7   ♠ 6 3
♡ 8 5 3   ♡ K 7 6 2
◊ Q J 5 4 2   ◊ A 10 8
♣ Q J 10 3   ♣ A 9 7 2

♠ A K Q J 10 8
♡ A J 4
◊ K 3
♣ 8 5

WEST	NORTH	EAST	SOUTH
			1♠
pass	2♠	pass	4♠
all pass			

West leads the ♣Q against your spade game. You play low from dummy and duck again when the ♣J is continued. West leads a third round of clubs to the king and ace. How will you play the hand?

You must ruff with a high trump, preserving your ♠8 as a means of entering the dummy. You then draw trumps with the ace and nine, employing your sole entry to the dummy. You need to find East with both the ♡K and the ◊A. Even if this is the case, how can you arrange the play to take the various finesses necessary?

You should lead the ♡Q. If East covers with the ♡K, everything will be easy. You can re-enter dummy with the ♡10 to lead a diamond towards your hand. Suppose instead that East plays low. You should unblock the ♡J from your hand. You continue with the ♡10. Again, if East covers, you will be able to re-enter dummy in hearts. If he plays low instead, you can underplay with your ♡4 (thanks to the previous unblock of the ♡J). You will remain in dummy for a lead towards your ◊K.

Note that it would not be good enough to run the ♡10 on the first round. East could then cover the ♡Q with the ♡K and you would not be able to return to the dummy to lead towards the ◊K.

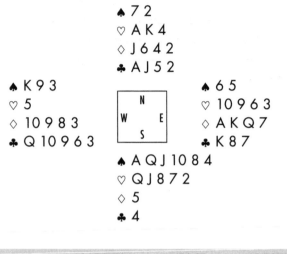

	♠ 7 2	
	♡ A K 4	
	◇ J 6 4 2	
	♣ A J 5 2	
♠ K 9 3		♠ 6 5
♡ 5		♡ 10 9 6 3
◇ 10 9 8 3		◇ A K Q 7
♣ Q 10 9 6 3		♣ K 8 7
	♠ A Q J 10 8 4	
	♡ Q J 8 7 2	
	◇ 5	
	♣ 4	

WEST	NORTH	EAST	SOUTH
			1♠
pass	2♣	pass	2♡
pass	3◇ *	pass	3♡
pass	4♡	all pass	

As it happens, 4♠ would have been more comfortable. Anyway, West
leads the ◇ 10 against your heart game. You ruff the diamond continuation, cross to the ♡A and finesse the ♠Q. West wins with the king and
forces you again with a third round of diamonds. What now?

You are down to three trumps. If the defenders' trumps break 3-2
you can draw them and score an overtrick. To succeed against a 4-1
trump break, you should instead play your spade winners. As the cards
lie, both defenders follow to the second spade. You play a third spade,
discarding dummy's last diamond, and the contract is secure. East ruffs
and plays another diamond but you ruff with dummy's ♡K (to avoid
blocking the trump suit). You can then lead the ♡4 to your ♡Q, draw
trumps and claim ten tricks.

It may seem that you are catering for a 4-1 trump break at the expense of losing to a 4-1 spade break (when trumps are 3-2). However, you will not necessarily go down when the spades are 4-1. Suppose that East started with only one spade. He would ruff the second spade and force you yet again in diamonds. You would still survive when East had started with three trumps rather than two. You could ruff with the ♡J, draw the two outstanding trumps with your bare ♡Q and run the remaining spades.

Problem 33

```
        ♠ 9 2
        ♡ 8 5
        ◇ K 7 6 5 4 3 2
        ♣ 8 6
♣3 led
        ♠ A J 4
        ♡ A Q 7 4
        ◇ A 10 8
        ♣ K Q 5
```

WEST	NORTH	EAST	SOUTH
			2NT
pass	3NT	all pass	

You reach 3NT and West leads the ♣3, East playing the ♣10. How will you play the contract?

Problem 34

```
        ♠ 10 9 7 3
        ♡ 5 2
        ◇ 10 3 2
        ♣ A J 9 2
♠K led
        ♠ A
        ♡ A K Q J 10 9 7
        ◇ 9 7 6 4
        ♣ K
```

WEST	NORTH	EAST	SOUTH
		3◇	4♡
all pass			

East opens with a preemptive 3◇ and you overcall 4♡ because you are too strong to bid just 3♡. How will you play the heart game when West leads the ♠K?

Problem 35

♠ 10 8 3
♡ K Q 10 2
◇ 7 5
♣ Q J 8 3

◇ 2 led

♠ A K 5
♡ J 9 4
◇ A K Q J 10 6
♣ A

WEST	NORTH	EAST	SOUTH
			2♣
pass	2NT	pass	6◇
all pass			

You have always thought that three bids were enough to reach a slam. How will you play the contract when West leads a low trump?

Problem 36

♠ Q 3
♡ 5
◇ A K 9 8 5 3 2
♣ 8 6 3

♣ 2 led

♠ A 6
♡ A K Q J 10 6
◇ 7
♣ A K 7 5

WEST	NORTH	EAST	SOUTH
			2♣
3♠	4◇	pass	6♡
all pass			

Three bids by your side are once again enough to reach a slam. How will you play 6♡ when West leads the ♣2 and East plays the ♣9?

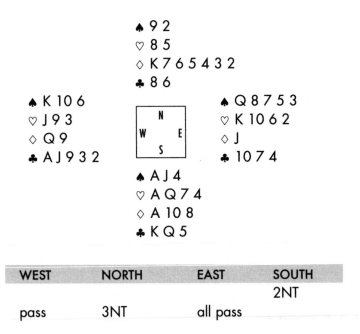

♠ 9 2
♡ 8 5
◇ K 7 6 5 4 3 2
♣ 8 6

♠ K 10 6   ♠ Q 8 7 5 3
♡ J 9 3   ♡ K 10 6 2
◇ Q 9   ◇ J
♣ A J 9 3 2   ♣ 10 7 4

♠ A J 4
♡ A Q 7 4
◇ A 10 8
♣ K Q 5

WEST	NORTH	EAST	SOUTH
			2NT
pass	3NT	all pass	

West leads the ♣3 against 3NT, East playing the ♣10. A hold-up in clubs can gain only when clubs are 6-2 and this is excluded by the opening lead of a three-spot. So, you win the first trick. What now?

Even if diamonds break 2-1, the suit is in danger of being blocked on the third round. To avoid a blockage you will have to duck the first or second round of diamonds. On the present deal you would like to duck this trick to West, so that the clubs are still protected. Should you lead the ◇10, intending to duck the first round, or play ace and another diamond, planning to duck the second round?

Both lines work when West holds ◇Q-J or ◇Q-J-9. Ducking the first round succeeds also when West holds a singleton ◇Q (not when he holds a singleton ♡J, since East can then overtake). Playing ace and another diamond will succeed when West holds ◇Q-9 or ◇J-9. So, it is twice as good in the cases where your play will make a difference. You should therefore win the first round of clubs and continue with ace and another diamond, ducking the second round when West plays the ◇Q.

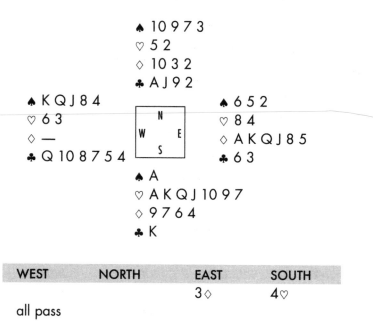

♠ 10 9 7 3
♡ 5 2
◊ 10 3 2
♣ A J 9 2

♠ K Q J 8 4
♡ 6 3
◊ —
♣ Q 10 8 7 5 4

♠ 6 5 2
♡ 8 4
◊ A K Q J 8 5
♣ 6 3

♠ A
♡ A K Q J 10 9 7
◊ 9 7 6 4
♣ K

WEST	NORTH	EAST	SOUTH
		3◊	4♡

all pass

How would you play this contract when West leads the king of spades?

You would like to score seven heart tricks and three top winners in the black suits. Unfortunately your club winners are blocked and there is no side entry to dummy that will allow you to untangle them. It is obvious from the bidding that diamonds are breaking 6-0. How can you take advantage of this knowledge? You suspect that West holds the ♠K-Q-J. If he also holds the ♣Q, which is a certainty after East's pre-empt on a 10-point suit, you will be able to endplay him.

After winning the spade lead, draw trumps in two rounds. You then overtake your king of clubs with the ace and lead the ♠10, discarding a diamond from your hand. West wins with the ♠J and, of course, has no diamond to play. Suppose he plays the ♠Q. You will discard another diamond from your hand. If West then plays the ♣Q, you will throw another diamond. He will then have to give the lead to dummy in one of the black suits. West's only alternative is to lead a low club instead. There is no guess involved because if East holds the ♣Q you cannot make the contract. You will therefore rise with dummy's ♣J. Since you can throw one diamond on this trick and another on the established ♠9, you will score an overtrick!

(Even if West started with ♡8-x-x, the alternative plan of throwing him in with the third round of trumps will not succeed against best defense. West will unblock the ♡8 on the first or second round.)

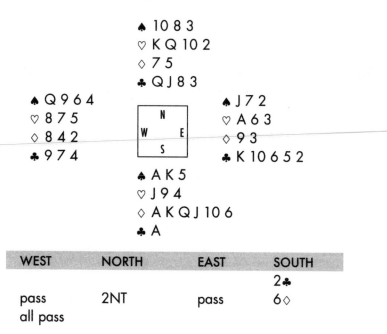

	♠ 10 8 3	
	♡ K Q 10 2	
	◇ 7 5	
	♣ Q J 8 3	

♠ Q 9 6 4		♠ J 7 2
♡ 8 7 5	N	♡ A 6 3
◇ 8 4 2	W E	◇ 9 3
♣ 9 7 4	S	♣ K 10 6 5 2

	♠ A K 5
	♡ J 9 4
	◇ A K Q J 10 6
	♣ A

WEST	NORTH	EAST	SOUTH
			2♣
pass	2NT	pass	6◇
all pass			

Giving up your claim for any bidding prize, you blast into the most likely contract on the second round. How will you play 6◇ when West leads a low trump?

Suppose you simply draw trumps and then play on hearts. Unless the ♡A is doubleton, the defenders will surely hold up the ace until the third round. You will then have no way to dispose of your spade loser. Instead you should draw trumps, cash the ♣A and overtake the jack of hearts with the king. If East captures this, you will have three heart tricks, enough for the contract. If he holds off, you will be in dummy and can lead the ♣Q for a ruffing finesse. If East follows with a low club, you will discard your spade loser. If instead he covers with the ♣K, you will ruff in your hand and lead a heart to the ♡10. Whether or not East takes his ace on this round, you are guaranteed a further entry to dummy. You will be able to throw your spade loser on the established club jack.

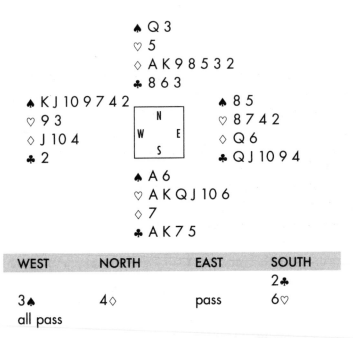

♠ Q 3
♡ 5
◇ A K 9 8 5 3 2
♣ 8 6 3

♠ K J 10 9 7 4 2
♡ 9 3
◇ J 10 4
♣ 2

♠ 8 5
♡ 8 7 4 2
◇ Q 6
♣ Q J 10 9 4

♠ A 6
♡ A K Q J 10 6
◇ 7
♣ A K 7 5

WEST	NORTH	EAST	SOUTH
			2♣
3♠	4◇	pass	6♡
all pass			

West leads the ♣2. You found no difficulty in bidding the slam, it's true, but will you be able to make it? You can discard the spade loser on the ◇K, so a 3-3 club break would give you the contract. That is somewhat unlikely, though, particularly after the ♣2 lead.

If diamonds break 3-2 you will be able to set up the suit. Unfortunately there will be no entry to dummy to enjoy the long cards. Or will there? If you are familiar with the more exotic bridge problems, you may have spotted how you can give yourself a chance of reaching dummy later in the play. Win the club lead and draw trumps in four rounds.

Next you should play your other top club. When West shows out you know for sure that the suit cannot break evenly. You cross to the ◇A and play the ◇K, making the spectacular discard of the ♠A. A diamond ruff sets up the suit and West now has nothing but spades in his hand. When you lead the ♠6 towards dummy, West cannot stop you from reaching dummy with the ♠Q. If he puts in the ♠K he will have to lead a spade to the next trick.

AFTERWORD

So, the entertainment draws to a close. We enjoyed writing the book and we very much hope that you enjoyed reading it. Was the effort worth your while? Of course it was! Study some dusty tome on double squeezes and you may have to wait weeks or months before you can put your acquired knowledge into practice. Entry Management will be involved, to some extent, in almost every contract that you play. Understanding the subject from declarer's point of view will also assist your defense. So, even if your reaction to the book is 'Sorry, but I found it rather hard work', your time has not been wasted. Next time you venture to a card table you may see some of the deals in a new light.

THE 'TEST YOUR BRIDGE TECHNIQUE' SERIES

Elimination Plays
Planning in Suit Contracts
The Simple Squeeze
Entry Management
Planning in Notrump Contracts
Endplays and Coups
Defending Suit Contracts
Safety Plays
Avoidance Play
Reading the Cards
Defending Notrump Contracts
Deceptive Play

Master Point Press
416-781-0351
www.masterpointpress.com
Email: info@masterpointpress.com